ABU DHABI

A PICTORIAL TOUR

Published with the support
and encouragement of

ABU DHABI

A PICTORIAL TOUR

MOTIVATE
PUBLISHING

Published by Motivate Publishing

Abu Dhabi: PO Box 43072, Abu Dhabi, UAE
Tel: (+971) 2 627 1666, fax: (+971) 2 627 1566

Dubai: PO Box 2331, Dubai, UAE
Tel: (+971) 4 282 4060, fax: (+971) 4 282 7593
e-mail: books@motivate.ae   www.booksarabia.com

Office 508, Building No 8, Dubai Media City, Dubai, UAE
Tel: (+971) 4 390 3550, fax: (+971) 4 390 4845

London: Acre House, 11/15 William Road, London NW1 3ER
e-mail: motivateuk@motivate.ae

Researched and written by Pippa Sanderson

| Directors: | Obaid Humaid Al Tayer |
| | Ian Fairservice |

Senior Editor:	David Steele
Editor:	Pippa Sanderson
Deputy Editor:	Jennifer Evans
Assistant Editor:	Zelda Pinto
Art Director:	Andrea Willmore
Book Publishing Manager:	Jeremy Brinton

© Motivate Publishing 1998 and 2006

First published 1998
Second edition 2006

ISBN: 1 86063 178 9

British Library Cataloguing-in-Publication Data. A catalogue record for this book is
available from the British Library.

Printed by Rashid Printers & Stationers LLC, Ajman, UAE.

INTRODUCTION

It is my pleasure to introduce *Abu Dhabi – A Pictorial Tour* to you and, if you are a visitor to our emirate, *Ahlan wa Sahlan* – welcome. This book presents a fascinating portrait of Abu Dhabi: it is a story and photographic record of the place and its people and captures the vital features of the city's history, character, achievements and phenomenal pace of development.

The pride the people have in their island city and emirate is clearly evident and I am pleased to note this book records their progress – and the involvement and influence of the people and their leaders. It is all of these people who've made history and, here in Abu Dhabi, history has been made on a grand scale.

Since the 1970s, Abu Dhabi has experienced extraordinary growth, thanks primarily to the visionary leadership of HH the late President, Sheikh Zayed bin Sultan Al Nahyan, whose legacy now lives on under the stewardship of his son, the new Ruler of Abu Dhabi and President of the UAE, Sheikh Khalifa bin Zayed Al Nahyan. Today, the city and emirate stand as a model of success, progress and tolerance – although their roots are still beautifully retained in the architecture of the city and the national dress, as reflected in the pages that follow.

Visitors to the city are inevitably struck by its many contrasts. The discovery of oil has brought

major advances – modern vehicles, high-rise buildings and international cultures that are a part of this book – yet equally, tradition retains its place in our daily lives. Indeed, the more Abu Dhabi progresses, the more it embraces its heritage – which is perhaps the main reason why it has remained so stable despite the rapid pace of development.

The result is an intriguing mix of old and new. While the capital city boasts some of the most impressive buildings in the Middle East, wooden dhows are still being built in their shadows. Fully equipped 4x4s head for the desert every weekend, but the Liwa retains its essential mystery and emptiness. Al Ain stands in the middle of a beautiful desert, yet it has been a successful community at the crossroads of major trade routes for almost 5,000 years.

Under Sheikh Zayed, the harsh, arid desert was 'greened' and subsequently, Abu Dhabi is now widely known as the 'Garden City of the Gulf' – as Al Ain is recognised as the 'Oasis City'. Few people, 30 years ago, would have believed this region could support such an abundance of trees and flowers.

As we watch Abu Dhabi grow into one of the most important cultural and economic centres in the Middle East, we all share in the keen awareness of what this wonderful city and emirate have come to represent in their unique blend of modernity, history and heritage.

It is a progression of knowledge, beliefs and accomplishments from generation to generation, and embodies the individual and collective wisdom and example of those who have lived in this land and been guided by the wisdom of our leaders.

And, if our past, our heritage and our present are any pointers to our future, Abu Dhabi will continue to reflect the unique and dynamic character that's guided its development over the years. All of us who live and work in Abu Dhabi are proud to be part of that spirit.

The myriad faces of Abu Dhabi are what makes it so special. As you look through the pages and the wonderful photographs in this book, which offer a privileged insight into the land and its people, we hope we succeed in encouraging you to venture out and discover even more of its beauty for yourself.

Abdullah bin Zayed Al Nahyan

The United Arab Emirates is a federation of seven emirates, consisting of Abu Dhabi, Dubai, Sharjah, Ajman, Umm al-Qaiwain, Fujairah and Ra's al-Khaimah. The Emirate of Abu Dhabi, home to the country's capital city, covers an area of 67,300 square kilometres, by far the largest of the seven. The capital city of Abu Dhabi lies to the north, with the industrial town of Ruwais to the west and the oasis city of Al Ain to the east. The southern part of the emirate is characterized by giant sand dunes and those in the Liwa and the Rub al-Khali (The Empty Quarter) are among the highest in the world. Despite its popularity with modern off-road enthusiasts, this area remains a lonely place and was once regarded by the ancients as the edge of civilization. Harsh and unforgiving, particularly when sandstorms – or *shamals* – reduce visibility to zero, it's difficult to believe anything could live and survive here.

Abu Dhabi was founded in 1761 by Sheikh Dhiyab bin Isa, after a freshwater spring was found on the island. However, it has a history that stretches back many thousands of years. Excavations by the Abu Dhabi Island Archaeological Survey (ADIAS), the Al Ain Department of Antiquities and Tourism and foreign teams have identified sites that date back to the Late Stone Age and beyond, indicating that the inhabitants of this area have depended on the resources of the sea, the resources of the desert and its oases, and trading, to make a living for at least 5,000 years. These buildings, in the Jimi Oasis in Al Ain are, of course, more recent examples of traditional architecture, but they still provide a fascinating link with the past.

When he came to power in 1966, one of the most urgent tasks for Sheikh Zayed bin Sultan Al Nahyan was the improvement of links between the island of Abu Dhabi and the mainland. In 1968, work began on the construction of Al-Maqta'a Bridge to replace the old causeway. The bridge, now with a twin beside it, is an essential part of the road network.

Above: As capital city of the Emirates, Abu Dhabi island has always been closely guarded. Visitors would usually cross Al-Maqta'a causeway, formerly the sole crossing point at low tide. They would also pass by the ancient watchtower which was manned in earlier, more combative, times.

Left: At the centre of the island is the ruler's fort, Qasr al-Hosn. The oldest building in Abu Dhabi, it was built in 1795 to enclose the original freshwater source said to have been found by tribesmen hunting a gazelle. The fort remained the ruling family's seat of power, and home, until 1966, and is still protected by spiked wooden doors. Old aerial photographs show it as the only building in what has since become the perennially busy area where Hamdan Street meets Al-Nasr Street. Now encircled by countless tall buildings, it remains a dignified landmark.

15

Above: Qasr al-Hosn shares its grounds with the Cultural Foundation, one of the most important buildings in Abu Dhabi. A modern edifice redolent of an earlier age, it has an archive, library, exhibition hall, theatre, cinema and meeting rooms, all of which are open to visitors. It also hosts several cultural events each year, including concerts and film screenings, art exhibitions and workshops.

Left: The Sheikh Zayed bin Sultan Al Nahyan Mosque, known locally as the Grand Mosque. One of the largest mosques in the world and covering an area of more than 22,000-square metres, it is located on the outskirts of the city, near to Al-Maqta'a Bridge. It is the final resting place for its namesake, the late President of the United Arab Emirates, who died in November 2004.

Abu Dhabi's traditions and social history are recreated in several working exhibits at the city's Heritage Village located along the Breakwater. Most interesting is the mosque (pictured left) and traditional *'arish* houses, ingenious dwellings that used windtowers to stay cool in the days before air-conditioning. Camels, donkeys, goats, handicrafts and recreations of a traditional souk and a well (pictured above) are also on display.

Dhow builders at the Bateen Yard on the western side of the island, above, employ centuries-old techniques. The arrival of modern dhows, left, has not harmed their craft, which has been kept alive by ongoing interest in the region's cultural heritage and by the fishermen and dhow racers who prefer their boats hand-built using traditional methods.

Following spread: The Dhow Harbour at Mina Zayed offers another taste of the past, with its floating village of traditional, wooden dhows. Pictured is a dhow festooned with *gargours* (fish traps) and the more mundane necessities required for long periods at sea.

Traditional Arabian dancing presents an evocative sight. There are some 10 genres, each with distinct identities; the most popular being the *ayyalah*, or stick dance, a re-enactment of a battle scene that originated as a response to danger. Tribesmen would sound their drums and shout, before repelling an attack. Youngsters take part in the dance too, typically walking along the front of the line of men, spinning their wooden rifles aloft.

Born to a desert environment, camels have been intrinsically linked with man in this part of the world since the dromedaries were first domesticated around 1300–1200 BC. Camel races, held each Thursday and Friday through the cooler months, are a celebration of that bond and are part of the region's heritage. Combining the excitement of the world's great horse races with the unique flavour of the Arab World, big money is often at stake and champion racing camels can fetch several million dirhams at auction. The photograph on the left was taken at Al Ain's atmospheric camel market.

Falconry is an enduring sport throughout the United Arab Emirates, passed on through the generations of Bedouin hunters who caught houbara bustards and desert hares to supplement their diet. Although hunting is now taboo, the skills are kept alive, and falcons are often an Emirati's most prized possession. Peregrines and sakers are trained to respond to their masters' voices, learning to catch prey by chasing a *tilwah* or lure, swung on the end of a rope.

From the unforgiving vastness of the desert evolved the oldest known breed of riding horse in the world – the Arabian – honed zealously by the Bedouin for thousands of years for its intelligence, speed and endurance; and the birth of a foal is cause for great celebration. As prized possessions, the Prophet Mohammed (PBUH) is believed to have decreed that those who nurtured the horse would reap their reward for such after death. Arabians are so athletic and distinctive that many of history's most feared and favoured warriors rode them, including Alexander the Great, Genghis Khan, Napoleon and George Washington.

A saluki in a winter's morning mist (above). Along with the camel, falcon and Arabian horse, the saluki is another traditional creature of Arabia, prized for its excellent hunting skills, its speed and agility. Known as the Gazelle Hound, the elegant saluki was the royal dog of Egypt and is one of the oldest breeds in the world, with pictures of the noble beast gracing Egyptian tombs dating back to 2100 BC. Regarded as a sacred gift from Allah, salukis were only ever offered as gifts; never sold.

Situated on a triangular island, Abu Dhabi is the federal capital of the United Arab Emirates. In just a few decades, the original small settlement has grown into a city of modern, high-rise towers, with parks, manicured public gardens and a sophisticated network of roads. (Courtesy Space Imaging Middle East.)

Offshore exploration, following surveys undertaken for British Petroleum by Commander Jacques Cousteau in 1954, led to the discovery of some of the most extensive oil and gas reserves in the region. The offshore fields are operated by Adma-Opco and Zadco, both part of the Abu Dhabi National Oil Company (Adnoc); along with foreign consortiums, including TotalFinaElf, whose giant platform is pictured left. It's estimated that Abu Dhabi has sufficient reserves to produce two-million barrels of oil a day for at least another 100 years.

Oil has transformed Abu Dhabi island and prompted an incredible construction boom. Where once only a handful of dwellings shared the land, hundreds of high-rise towers and a sophisticated network of roads have now appeared. Architecture in modern Abu Dhabi encompasses fluid design elements that are both surreal and aesthetically pleasing to the eye.

The construction of mirrored monoliths, fashioned from state-of-the-art materials to reflect and complement the more traditional Islamic styles surrounding them, has led to the city being dubbed the 'Manhattan of the Middle East'. Abu Dhabi continues to grow and evolve, a city of high-rise buildings juxtaposed with elegant mosques that offers an intriguing blend of the religious and the secular.

The city of Abu Dhabi was created from almost nothing in little more than three decades. Mosques mingle effortlessly with high-rise buildings, almost invariably built with mirrored glass to keep out the sun, and the result is an intriguing spectrum of colour and light. And, even during a rare thunder storm, the understated elegance of Abu Dhabi's mosques is unequivocal.

Above: Al-Ittihad Square near Abu Dhabi's Corniche, one of the city's remaining landmarks, includes a unique collection of giant cannon, incense burner, coffee pot (*dalla*) and perfume bottle.

Right: Abu Dhabi is designed on a grid, with roads signposted in Arabic and English, although few people are familiar with their numerical layout and many roads have more than one name. Traffic control remains a priority for city planners, hence the demise of most of the old roundabouts and the appearance of four-way junctions.

The wide vista afforded from the tops of Abu Dhabi's tallest buildings gives a whole new perspective to the city and the incredible development of this desert island can be appreciated in full. It's easy to forget that, just a few decades ago, this was nothing but barren, flat desert.

Wide, multi-laned roads ease movement round the capital. Pictured is the Sheraton Abu Dhabi Resort & Towers, one of the island's original five-star hotels. Overlooking the Arabian Gulf, the Sheraton is located within easy walking distance of the newly developed Corniche.

The city's interiors are a combination of form and function, with atriums and interiors providing an attractive respite from the constant sun. The Cultural Foundation, above, boasts large windows and arabesque flair, while the colours in Emirates Palace hotel's Grand Atrium dome, left, at 42-metres wide, reflect the different shades of sand found within the Arabian desert.

The Eastern Corniche (Corniche al-Qurm) overlooking the lagoon on the eastern side of the island is fringed with mangroves and white sandy shores. It's a popular spot for walkers, picnickers and bird watchers alike and offers a castellated promenade, shaded tables and a plethora of date palms, providing the perfect opportunity to gaze across the beautiful blue waters.

The Corniche al-Qurm's extensive mangroves provide food and shelter to an abundance of wildlife, such as egrets and herons. The skyline of the modern metropolis contrasts strongly, yet harmoniously, with this natural splendour.

Abu Dhabi's Corniche has enjoyed extensive changes during the past few decades and it is now one of the most modern in the world. The city's increasing importance as a business centre, not to mention its emerging tourist market, has led to the building of many new hotels, where a few decades ago there were none. The Baynunah Hilton Tower, left, once the tallest building in the Gulf, still dominates the skyline.

The Corniche stretches for eight kilometres along Abu Dhabi's north-west coast and it is one of the city's most enduring attractions. A multi-billion dirham facelift has resulted in the construction of several new buildings that encompass state-of-the-art design and facilities.

Above: The waters around Abu Dhabi are mostly shallow and ideal for swimming, but can prove troublesome for inexperienced sailors and their boats. Deeper channels have been dredged for vessels using the port and are marked by buoys on both sides, but care is still needed to avoid the sandbanks which are exposed at low tide. For this reason, few boats venture out after dark.

Left: Many residents are drawn to the Corniche at sunset, congregating under modern, canopied structures to watch the sun ebb away into twilight.

Much of Abu Dhabi island has been reshaped or created from new, such as the Breakwater that, with the opening of Marina Mall in 2001, became a focal point for shopping. The mall is being extended to include a 100-metre-high viewing tower offering patrons a 360-degree view of the city and sea.

Camel seats are unusual objects to purchase and testimony to the growing interest in local folk art, while the *mehbash* and *mahmas,* above, used to grind coffee in the desert, are increasingly sought after. Other souvenirs of Arabia, right, are available for purchase and make a fitting memento.

Following spread: Rugs from the Carpet Souk are usually machine-made reproductions, but the Centre for Traditional Iranian Carpets is thought, by some, to house the best collection in the world ouside Iran. Hundreds of designs are on display, exquisite hand-stitched examples from Tabriz, Isfahan and Qum. The costs for the finest rugs can be astronomical, but smaller *zaronim* carpets are more affordable in the United Arab Emirates than elsewhere and can be bought for as little as Dhs 3,000. The Carpet Souk sells woollen and silk rugs made in Turkey and Iran, among other countries, and is located at the end of the Corniche in the commercial sector.

Abu Dhabi and Al Ain are still market towns, less commercially orientated than Dubai, but commercial nevertheless. Proximity to the sea means fresh fish and shellfish are always available, but perhaps the freshest produce comes from the Emirate of Abu Dhabi itself. Date palms have been particularly successful and locally grown fruit and vegetables are a feature at the souk, including succulent water melons, left. Pictured above are clusters of dates, ripening quickly in the heat of summer.

The staple of the Arab diet has long been the date, a sweet-tasting fruit famed for its medicinal and nutritional value. Dates are often taken with coffee in a *majlis* and are sometimes handed round at business meetings or social gatherings. They grow extremely well in the local climate, with several different varieties being produced. A visit to the date market will reveal a number of different sizes, shades and tastes and most vendors will insist you sample a few before buying.

Above: Gold and silver are especially good buys and considerably cheaper than in many other parts of the world. Gold is sold by weight, with additional costs for craftsmanship; and some pieces are astonishingly ornate.

Right: Silver items include genuine Bedouin pieces, made by melting down the Maria Theresa thalers that were once the region's currency. Jewellery, such as the curved *khanjars* at the top of the photograph, are most evocative of the past. The stunning weapons below are *jambia*, Yemeni daggers.

Not all of Abu Dhabi's shopping looks to the past. Malls are appearing at a bewildering rate; modern-day souks that combine a wide variety of goods with the comfort of year-round air-conditioning. Marina Mall, Abu Dhabi Mall and the Madinat Zayed Centre are the largest, while others such as Al-Hosn Plaza and the Al-Hanah Centre provide smaller havens of shopping.

Above and next spread: Abu Dhabi, despite its modern buildings, is no concrete jungle. It is known as the 'Garden City of the Gulf', a city of parks and fountains, and millions of dirhams have been invested in a greening programme that began in the late 1960s with Sheikh Zayed.

Left: Marina Mall's impressive seagull-themed lobby with its intricate stained-glass skylight. The mall is one of the largest shopping malls in the city's retail arsenal and covers an area of some 125,000 square metres.

With the maturing and continual progression of the greening programme, new species have thrived where previously they might have struggled. Bougainvillea, frangipani, hibiscus, flame trees, jasmine and varieties of cacti have all blossomed alongside the ubiquitous palms that carpet the country. Numerous migratory birds adopt the area as their home during the cooler months, while others, such as ring-necked parakeets, can be found throughout the island all year round. It may be an inhospitable climate for four or five months every year, but as the greening continues, the flora and fauna around Abu Dhabi can only increase.

Weekends are for leisure, with Abu Dhabi's residents mingling with visitors from around the world on the uncrowded public beach and shaded grass area adjacent to the Hiltonia Beach Club along the Corniche.

Abu Dhabi is surrounded by islands, from larger ones such as Sa'adiyat, Lulu, Sir Bani Yas, Futaisi and Abu Abyad to countless, much smaller islets, and every weekend sees a flotilla of craft heading from the marinas out to their favourite spots. The desert-island picnic has become something of an institution; a chance to swim, sit in the sun, waterski or, for the more ecologically minded, explore the islands themselves. While some islands are really just exposed sandbanks, with very little in the way of vegetation, others provide a fascinating mix of mangrove swamp and corals. Home to numerous birds, insects and reptiles, some are also nesting sites for green and hawksbill turtles.

Abu Dhabi's Breakwater provides excellent opportunities to relax and unwind from the stresses of modern living, and the city's residents invest much time and energy in pursuing their interests there, whether it's messing about with boats, fishing or sitting on a bench and watching the world go by, especially during winter when many people spend their leisure time outside.

The Emirates Palace hotel, opened in 2005, is located at the start of the Breakwater and boasts a total of 114 domes atop the main and ancillary buildings. Its Grand Atrium, in the centre of the principal building, is 42-metres wide and has a surface of silver- and gold-coloured mosaic tiles.

Abu Dhabi International Airport, located on the mainland some 30 kilometres from the city, was opened in 1982, and replaced the original island-based Al-Bateen Airport that had been operational since 1968. Abu Dhabi Duty Free, opened in 1984, offers international, branded goods and is housed in a stunning complex. It is one of the finest duty-free shops in the world.

The desire to celebrate its past has influenced Abu Dhabi's sporting culture. Dhow sailing is one of the more spectacular examples and attracts huge crowds to the Corniche and Breakwater. Rowing boats, pictured, are also raced, sometimes on longer courses between the emirates. With up to 100 oarsmen in each vessel, competitors hail from different tribes and families.

The seas around the island are a playground for sports lovers. Jetskis are perhaps the easiest way of taking to the water and the channel between the InterContinental and Khalidia Palace beaches has become a favourite spot for riders to show off their tricks. Those in search of a different kind of action may prefer to head for the open seas and some rewarding big-game fishing.

Left: Abu Dhabi hosted the inaugural Abu Dhabi Golf Championship in January 2006, part of the European Golf Tour. Many of the top international golf stars took part, including Colin Montgomerie, pictured. American Chris DiMarco was the eventual winner.

Far left: The widespread interest in sport is hardly surprising; come winter, Abu Dhabi is the perfect place to be outdoors. For some, this might mean taking to the seas, while the temperature-controlled pools – cooled in summer, heated in winter – are an irresistable attraction to all.

Above: The unique Abu Dhabi World Sand Golf Championship attracts the world's top golf professionals, such as Paul McGinley, Nick Faldo and Padraig Harrington, pictured. It is held at the Al-Ghazal Golf Course and offers sculpted sand fairways and 'browns' instead of 'greens'.

Right: Golf has made an enormous impact in the UAE. The country boasts numerous grass courses, many of which have been honed to international standards. The Abu Dhabi Golf Club by Sheraton is one such course and comes complete with undulating fairways, pockets of palms, seven salt-water lakes and, at 350 metres, the longest driving range in the Gulf.

Abu Dhabi's numerous stables are testimony to the passion for equine pursuits in the Arab World – both flat, above, and endurance racing, left.

Much of Abu Dhabi's history has been about overcoming the elements and making an inhospitable environment as comfortable as possible. The least experienced amateur can now take to the sands in an off-road vehicle, conquering land which could once only be crossed by camel, although the sands can still catch out the over-confident and those who fail to treat the desert with the respect it deserves. Competitors in the annual UAE Desert Challenge have turned traversing the desert into a professional sport, but the majority of off-roaders are amateur enthusiasts keen to experience the silence of the desert for the weekend.

Opportunities for sporting spectators are excellent. Formula One and offshore powerboat races are among the sporting calendar's more glamorous fixtures and, thanks to the efforts of the Abu Dhabi International Marine Sports Club, Abu Dhabi has, in recent years, been host to the Formula One season's prestigious final race, where the action is always spectacular. Boating is by no means restricted to the professionals. Many residents have their own craft and enjoy state-of-the-art mooring facilities at the Inter-Continental, Mina Zayed, Marine Sports Club and Marina Club.

The Red Bull Air Race, a spectacular series spanning three continents, is a combination of slalom, motor-racing and acrobatics. Pilots must fly between pairs of 18-metre-high, air-filled cones as fast as they can, while performing aerobatic sequences, such as the Knife-Edge Crossing and Half Cuban Eight, all within a large rectangular arena measuring some 1,400 x 400 metres in size. Pictured in the foreground is Briton Nigel Lamb in his yellow plane with the eventual winner, Kirby Chambliss, coming up behind in the blue aircraft.

American Kirby Chambliss beat 10 peers in front of thousands of spectators who lined the Corniche in 2006 to watch both plane and pilot execute a series of manoeuvres, at times in excess of 400 kph. Prizes were awarded by, from left to right, Mohammed bin Barrak, member of the Abu Dhabi Tourism Authority, Sheikh Mohammed bin Butti Al Hamad, Abu Dhabi Ruler's Representative in the Western Region, and Moubarak Hamad Al Muheiri, Director General of the Abu Dhabi Tourism Authority.

Some 91 per cent of Abu Dhabi remains a wilderness of desert and salt flats (*sabkha*). Wind and occasional rainfall make for a subtly shifting landscape, a breathtaking sculpture of the elements and, for many, this represents Arabia in its most beautiful, natural state. The desert is also home to more than 50 species of reptile, such as the spiny-tailed lizard – known locally as the *dhab*, left – and the blue-headed agama, above.

The Arabian Peninsula is home to 14 species or sub-species of scorpion. In sandy areas, the most common is *Buthacus yotvatensis nigroaculeatus*, above. A fully grown specimen can reach some 75 mm. It has a yellow body except for the last segment of its tail and sting, which is black. *Androctonus crassicauda*, right, is one of the largest scorpions in the UAE, with a black body and chunky claws. Interestingly, all scorpions fluoresce in ultra-violet light and this phenomenon makes for easy detection, especially at night.

Above and next spread: It was a hunting party from the Liwa, on the trail of a gazelle, which is believed to have discovered water on the island of Abu Dhabi in the mid-18th century. Fresh water was a vital and scarce resource and Sheikh Dhiyab bin Isa, the paramount sheikh, ordered that a settlement be established in the place he called Abu Dhabi, or 'father of the gazelle'.

Thanks to HH Sheikh Zayed bin Sultan Al Nahyan and his commitment to conservation on Sir Bani Yas Island and at Al Ain Zoo among others, many endangered animal species have been saved from extinction, including the Arabian oryx pictured. The number of Arabian and sand gazelles are also increasing, along with hares and desert foxes.

Above: Sodom's Apple, a member of the milkweed family. Goats and camels steer clear of this plant because of its poisonous milk. The latex, with its medicinal properties, was traditionally used to treat wounds and skin afflictions.

Left: Abu Dhabi's *sabkha* flats transform into sandy plains that are scattered with halophyte vegetation, plants adapted to survive in very saline conditions, which store salt in the fluids enclosed within their globular leaves.

Following spread: The heat of the sun has quickly dried this large pool of mud, situated in a depression between dunes not far from Al Ain, and the resulting cracks have created interesting abstract patterns.

Above, left and following spread: For five millennia, Al Ain – the Oasis City – has thrived at the foot of the magnificent Hajar Mountains, rocky peaks which stand astride the UAE and Oman. Jebel Hafit, the highest point in the Emirate of Abu Dhabi, provides some of the most spectacular scenery in the region and is a popular destination for tourists.

With its ancient tombs and archaeological remains, Jebel Hafit is a mythical place of *djinns* (supernatural spirits) from Arabic folklore, and one of the highlights of Al Ain. Slightly daunting, especially at night, the *jebel* rises dramatically to some 1,180 metres above sea level and affords spectacular views of the wadis, oases and plains below. Easily reached via a long, meandering road, it makes an impressive, if somewhat incongruous, sight.

Above and right: Hili Archaeological Gardens suggests that the Al Ain area was inhabited as long as 5,000 years ago – one of the oldest settlements in the United Arab Emirates. The Bronze Age settlement, above, and graves, right, were excavated by a Danish team in the 1960s and have since been the subject of extensive work by the emirate's own achaeological teams. Many of these fascinating artefacts can now be seen in the Al Ain Museum.

Next spread: Al-Jahli Fort is the birthplace of the late UAE President, Sheikh Zayed. One of several fortresses found in Al Ain, it was built in 1898 by Sheikh Zayed the Great and is one of the country's foremost landmarks.

Above: Many fine examples of Islamic architecture exist in Abu Dhabi. Nowhere is this more true than in the doors, arches and battlements of its fortifications, especially those at Al-Jahli Fort, which served to protect the hamlet's inhabitants in less harmonious times.

Left: Al Ain, literally meaning 'the spring', has long been able to exploit its reserves of subterranean water using *falaj* (irrigation) channels. In the past, they were privately owned, managed by officials, or *arifs*, who charged *masha* taxes for their upkeep, but modern pipelines mean the *falaj* is no longer as essential for survival as it once was.

The farms in the vicinity of Abu Dhabi and Al Ain provide an abundance of fruit and vegetables, with the more delicate crops cultivated under 'plastika' tunnels that provide added protection against the sun.

Above: The annual Al Ain Flower Show & Festival is redolent with a riot of floral colour during the week-long festival. Including displays of one million flowers along roads, roundabouts and in parks throughout the city, the show is not merely an exercise in temporary beautification, but also highlights global best practices in horticulture.

Left: Activities during the five-day annual Al Ain Air Show include daring aerobatic displays from various types of aircraft. One of the highlights in the 2006 event included the setting of a new world record, that of a group of 54 intrepid skydivers from 16 countries, who jumped together and linked up at 3,962 metres (13,000 feet).

Above: The Liwa is a long, crescent-shaped series of oasis settlements located 240 kilometres south of the city of Abu Dhabi at the edge of the Rub al-Khali, or The Empty Quarter. It is the historical home of the Bani Yas confederation of tribes, of which the Abu Dhabi ruling family – the Al Nahyans – are part.

Right: The recently renovated Attab Fort in the Liwa Crescent, some 55 kilometres from Hameem. The fort is set back from a modern dual carriageway, a smooth tarmac thoroughfare that follows the old tracks that connected many of the small hamlets along the crescent.

Above: The Jabbana Fort in the Liwa Crescent, which has also been renovated. The fortress can be found behind a row of shops just off the main Liwa dual carriageway.

Left and right: As much as the modern capital city of Abu Dhabi has to offer, for many it's a trip back to the simpler times of yesteryear, along with the starkness of the desert that holds the greatest appeal.

Above: With a 4x4 and a few basic survival skills, weekends in the spectacular sand dunes of The Empty Quarter are a great way to unwind away from the city and escape the madding crowd.

Left: The Empty Quarter does not contain only vast sand dunes, but large areas of *sabkha* too. Arabic for salt flats, *sabkha* are flat, very saline expanses of sand or silt, formed by the evaporation of sub-surface moisture.

The beauty of The Empty Quarter to the south of the emirate, which extends
deep into Saudi Arabia and Oman, is revealed in all its glory during sunrise
and sunset. Its many intricate sand patterns are in a constant state of flux,
hostages to the whim of the warm desert breezes.

141

Sir Bani Yas Island is a lush haven of tranquillity, located 170 kilometres to the west of Abu Dhabi. More than 30 archaeological sites have been identified on the island, one of the most important being a Christian Nestorian monastery and church that date back to the sixth to seventh-centuries AD. In contemporary times, Sir Bani Yas Island was completely transformed by Sheikh Zayed bin Sultan Al Nahyan and his environmental initiative to breed endangered species, and plant trees. Roaming freely around the island are blackbuck, sand gazelle, mountain gazelle, Arabian oryx, ostrich and desert hare among others, while, pictured left, the island's palace and its surrounding lawn stretch right down to the water's edge.

Previous spread: An overview of Sir Bani Yas Island from one of its highest points, with the island's new hotel pictured in the distance.

Acknowledgements

The publishers would like to thank all the photographers who contributed their memorable images for this book, and Peter Hellyer for his invaluable advice. Thanks also go to Mubadala Development, without whose encouragement and support the publication of this book would not have been possible.

PHOTOGRAPHIC CREDITS

Abu Dhabi Airport:	94
Abu Dhabi Golf Club by Sheraton:	94/95
Al Ain Flower Show & Festival:	131
Aufschnaiter, Stefan:	85
Dumont, Nicolas:	103
Emirates Palace Hotel:	46
Gardi, Balazs:	102
Gulf Images:	1
Motivate Publishing:	Back cover, 17, 47, 86, 86/87
Newington, Greg:	Front cover, 5, 6/7, 14/15, 16/17, 19, 22/23, 41, 42, 44, 52, 53, 56/57, 58/59, 64/65, 74/75, 80/81, 82, 83, 90, 100/101, 140/141, 142, 143
Salik, Farooq:	93, 130B
Shankar, Adiseshan:	57, 60, 66/67, 69
Sanderson, Pippa:	2, 11, 15, 18, 24, 25, 26, 27, 28, 30, 31T&B, 35, 36, 38, 39, 40, 42/43, 45, 48, 48/49, 61, 68, 70, 72, 78/79, 84, 88/89, 92, 96, 97, 104, 105, 106T&B, 107, 108/109, 112, 116, 117, 122, 126, 128, 129, 132, 133, 136, 137
Space Imaging Middle East:	32/33
Steele, David:	8/9, 10/11, 12/13, 20/21, 21, 37, 50/51, 54/55, 62/63, 65, 71, 73, 76, 77, 91, 110/111, 113, 114/115, 118/119, 120/121, 122/123, 124/125, 127, 135
Steele, Mark:	130T
Total Communications:	98, 99
TotalFinaElf:	34/35
Willmore, Andrea:	134T&B, 138, 139
Zandi, Dariush:	29

T: top; B: bottom